Storytelling

How To Tell Amazing Stories And Inspire Your Audience

(Public Speaking, Communication, Ted Talks)

by Dean Coleman

© 2016 Dean Coleman
All Rights Reserved

Table of Contents

Table of Contents

Introduction

Chapter 1 – Beginning With The Basics: An Essential Primer Kit for Public Speaking

Chapter 2 – The Monomyth Explained: A Storytelling Template That Has Survived the Test of Time

Chapter 3 – The Power of the Senses: Using Words To Paint Pictures in Your Audience's Heads

Conclusion

Disclaimer

While all attempts have been made to verify the information provided in this book, the author does not assume any responsibility for errors, omissions, or contrary interpretations of the subject matter contained within. The information provided in this book is for educational and entertainment purposes only. The reader is responsible for his or her own actions and the author does not accept any responsibilities for any liabilities or damages, real or perceived, resulting from the use of this information.

Introduction

"Goddess, daughter of Zeus, speak, and begin our story."

—Homer, calling on the divine powers of the Muse to guide him through his oral performance of The Odyssey.

There's no contest: public speaking is mankind's most sacred tradition.

Before recorded history, skilled storytellers enjoyed status on par with the great warrior chieftains of their tribes.

In ancient Greece, the prestige of poet orators like Homer and Rhapsody was on par with that of the Oracles themselves. By many accounts, the average Greek saw little distinction between these early performers and the mystically-attributed priest caste of their day.

During medieval times—an age when even the most elite nobles battled and bled for their livelihoods—lowborn minstrels, bards, and troubadours enjoyed lives of relative comfort and security.

Once more, a beloved court jester lived in luxury beyond even the nobleman's wildest dreams, and many royal fools were held in such high regard that they had influence over the king himself.

And what of the "bards", "oral poets", and verbal "storytellers" of today? Today, public speaking is among the highest-earning professions in the world—if not *the* number one well-paid profession.

(For this, it depends on who you ask and what you consider public speaking. It's well known, for example, that Hillary Clinton makes millions of dollars at a time with so-called "speaking fees" from massive corporations.

Or course, many speculate that her fees pay for more than a rousing performance. Still, prolific public speakers like Tony Robbins and Dan S. Kennedy—people with no political power to leverage—are also known to command fees of several hundred-thousand dollars per appearance.)

But what to make of this unbelievable value that humanity has always assigned to public speaking?

First, make no mistake: the value of a storyteller extends far beyond the entertainment aspect of their craft. Yes, the unwashed masses adore "bread and circuses," as the Roman poet Juvenal so wisely noted.

But rest assured, a proficient storyteller provides so much more than mere fleeting amusement. A storyteller also holds great influence over his or her audience.

This principle is best exemplified in the "motivational speaker" subgenre of the modern-day storyteller. Think about how much each individual audience member pays for their ticket to a Tony Robbins motivational seminar (it's *a lot)*.

Trust me, they're not paying all that money to be entertained (if so, they have very expensive taste!), nor are they paying to learn something they don't already know.

After all, messages that essentially boil down to, "You need to work harder and love what you're doing" are hardly hidden knowledge. No, the people who attend these pricy seminars are *really* paying for something else.

They're really paying to be *changed*.

They're putting big dollars down on the bet that this one-time, one to three-hour event is going to positively alter the way they think and feel about themselves...forever.

And you know what? Much of the time, that bet pays off. Countless people agree that a Tony Robbins, Zig Ziglar or similar speaker's performance was a pivotal turning point in their lives.

And not only will they *tell you that*, but they also have the numbers (in the form of better sales figures, bigger clients for their business, lower blood pressure, lower body mass index, and so on) to back that statement up.

Such is the power of an effective public speaker with a message.

Whether your overall goal is to motivate your audience or simply to connect with them on a deeper level via heartfelt anecdote, this book will teach you how to utilize storytelling to your advantage. Let's get started.

Chapter 1 – Beginning With The Basics: An Essential Primer Kit for Public Speaking

Before we talk about how to spin a yarn that captivates your audience, it's important to lay some groundwork for public speaking in general. If you're already an experienced public speaker, you may find portions of this chapter somewhat redundant, but I highly recommend that you give it good skim regardless.

On the other hand, if you're new to public speaking, this chapter contains critical knowledge that can instantly take your performance to the next level. Don't miss out on these five public speaking tips for a professional-quality performance.

Public Speaking Pro Tip #1: Know Your Audience Like You Know Yourself, Then Speak to Them (In)Directly

Even the giants of the public speaking industry—Tony Robbins, Dan Kennedy, Zig Ziglar—would have their effectiveness greatly diminished if they were thrust before a crowd that's incompatible with their message or speaking style.

For the rest of us—those without decades of performing experience underneath our belts—a performance not tailored to our specific audience can be an absolute disaster.

So before you so much as consider the overall message of your speech, first consider your audience. Consider them very well.

Who are they? What's a day like in their shoes? What's the first thing they think about in the morning, and the last thing they think about at night? These aren't hypothetical questions. Really ask them to yourself. Even better, ask them to a person who represents your audience.

Then, begin to ask yourself more abstract things about your audience. Things such as:

What *moves* them? What makes them uncomfortable? What makes them happy? What would they need to hear for their eyes to swell up with tears of pride? For their skin to break out in goose pimples? For a shiver to run down their spine?

There's no universal answer to these questions, just like there's no universal audience, just like there's no universal *message*.

That's why you must tailor your speech accordingly. First profile your audience. Then decide exactly what it is you want to tell them—your speech's overall message. Make sure it suits them. Then summarize this into one concise sentence. Then trim that sentence down to core as much as humanly possible. Make it stupid simple.

Take these examples:

The stupid simple message of MLK's *I Have a Dream* speech is "Equality for all races in society."

The stupid simple message of Reagan's *Tear Down This Wall* speech is "End this oppressive regime."

Watch these famous speeches, and notice how each of their messages is relayed—at the peak moment of the speech—through potent metaphors.

A *dream* is a powerful word that's embroiled with positive feelings. A dream is more than a goal, it's a *dream*. It's a worthy ideal, a lofty proposition, and usually something far from reach. And yet, King's true message called for an immediate change in society. He only used the word *symbolically*.

Reagan's metaphor was much more specific: The Berlin Wall, a powerful token of an oppressive regime's toll on civil liberties. But at the same time, the wall itself was of little consequence.

It could have been bulldozed the day prior, but with the oppressive policies it represented still in place, the fact that the wall itself was now rubble would have meant nothing. Reagan used the wall to blast the policies.

Human beings have a strong affinity for metaphors like this. We're moved by *symbolic representation* because symbols affect us on intellectual *and* emotional level.

Why, after all, are metaphors so frequently employed in nearly all forms of communication? From causal conversation to pre-written speeches, from heated arguments to structured debates? It's because metaphors are stories in miniature. And stories speak to us *symbolically*.

With the matter of your audience and message both well in hand, you can confidently set your mind upon the *how*. That is to say, the task of how to deliver your message as effectively as possible.

Well, the most tried and true way to do that is through *symbolic representation*—storytelling—the subject of this book.

Public Speaking Pro Tip #2: Practice Creates *Confidence*, So Practice, Practice, Practice

The fear of public speaking is as natural as the fear of heights, the fear of enclosed spaces, and the fear of vaguely human-shaped figures leaping out from the shadows and attacking.

In other words, the fear of public speaking is a deep-set, DNA-bound, *instinctual fear*. Thankfully, the fear of public speaking can be greatly diminished through good old fashioned practice and preparation.

They say practice makes perfect. Well, when public speaking is concerned, my motto has always been: *forget about perfect.* Do yourself a favor and throw *perfect* out the window right this instant. There's no such thing as a perfectly delivered speech.

Even the most skilled and practiced public speaker trips over his tongue, loses his place, or fails to "hit the high note" of his speech from time to time. The pros gladly accept that these things will happen. It takes the weight of inhuman expectations off their shoulders, and it lets them perform more naturally.

No, when it comes to public speaking, practice is great because practice *creates confidence.*

It goes without saying that the sooner you begin rehearsing, the more confident you'll be when the day of your speech arrives. I've even worked with talented speakers who begin rehearsing a speech before they've even finished writing it!

That may seem counter-intuitive, but the act of verbalizing your speech before its finalized—and thus, hearing your ideas breathed into life out loud—helps refine your message as you write it.

Public Speaking Pro Tip #3: Speech Writing Has No Rules, Only Guidelines

On that note, a brief side tangent on speech writing in general. If you were drafting a novel, the previous paragraph's advice would be considered blasphemous to most well-studied writers. When drafting an essay or unspoken story, the conventional wisdom is to *not* edit as you write.

But speechwriting is a realm where conventional wisdom rarely applies.

Understand that a speech is perhaps the most profound and personal form of communication in the world. Unless you have a team of speech-writers and speech-coaches in the wing to craft your performance for you, your speech is a unique message from within—a well-polished product of your one-of-a-kind outlook and mentality.

When writing a speech, you really have to trust what you're doing because your speech is literally an expression of *you*.

To quote the great writer Steven Pressfield in his book, *Do The Work*:

"Trust the soup."

Trust the *what?* Here's what Pressfield means by this. When you sit down to draft your speech, and suddenly you find that your soul starts to pore out of your body and onto the page—all before you can so much as summarize your idea in bullet points format…just let it out. Let it flow. Don't fight it.

Understand that your subconscious mind is at work for you constantly in ways you're not aware. That's not airy fairy guru pep-talk, that's proven psychological fact. So don't resist whatever bubbles up from your subconscious when go to write your speech. Trust the soup.

Likewise, if you sit down to draft your speech and find that your story comes to you one chunk at a time, each block in demand of fine-tuning before the next block arrives: go with that as well. But in this regard don't sabotage yourself with the toxic myth of writer's block.

Push through the mental barriers until your speech is finished. To paraphrase another line from Pressfield's work: diamonds aren't scooped out of the sand with a shovel. They're very difficult to harvest.

All of that being said, when it comes to telling stories there's a certain structure—a loose set of guidelines, really—that humans find universally appealing and relatable. You'll learn how to fit your spoken stories into this structure during the next chapter.

Public Speaking Pro Tip #4: Emotional Cadence and Cantor – The Unspoken Subtext of Your Speech

If you yourself don't get emotionally involved in your speech, how can you expect your audience to?

A good speech delivery is a bit like a rollercoaster. It has peaks and valleys, anticipation and momentum. All of these things are communicated through your tone of voice, your pacing, and your overall body language.

The good news is: if you're speaking from the heart, these things should all come to you rather naturally. Most novices' problems with performing stem from inhibiting themselves too much.

Do yourself a favor and look up Charlie Chaplin's performance of "The Greatest Speech Ever Told" from his 1940 film, *The Great Dictator*. Hear the way his volume rises and falls; the way his rate of speaking gains pace as his message comes to head. Hear the way his voice quakes and falters during certain painful moments.

Don't get me wrong, you definitely don't need to reduce yourself to a blubbering mess on stage in order to deliver your message effectively. But you *should* strive to convey some level of personal vulnerability to your audience.

When you expose your inner workings to your audience, they become receptive to your message on the same sort of deeply personal wavelength.

Chapter 2 – The Monomyth Explained: A Storytelling Template That Has Survived the Test of Time

In the previous chapter, we briefly touched on the idea of "crescendos" in your speech. The idea that your delivery should never be stagnant, but vary as your performance unfolds. The idea that your speech should have a certain *rhythm*.

This concept also makes up the backbone of story-telling in general. If you embed the correct "emotional candor" into the content of your speech itself, an engaging delivery will naturally follow suit.

It just so happens, there's a hundred-thousand-year-old "template" for doing just that. It is a template for telling stories that speak to the essence of humanity.

Homer used it. Tolkien used it. George Lucas used it. Countless public speakers, politicians, and stand-up comedians the world over use it every day, and you can use it too.

I am speaking of what Joseph Campbell calls "The Monomyth." The monomyth describes a way to structure the plot of a story so that it engages and inspires an audience to great effect. Let's break it down.

How an Epic and Inspiring Hero's Journey Unfolds in Three Easy Acts

(Note: This is a highly condensed and streamlined version of the classical hero's journey outlined by the monomyth. For a full in-depth analysis, check out Joseph's Campbell's bestselling book *The Hero with a Thousand Faces*.)

ACT ONE: Our "Hero's tale" almost always begins with the protagonist in a slump. They're either bored to death with their hum-drum life or outright suffering in squalor.

Maybe they're not a very nice person, or maybe they are but they can't catch a break. Either way the gist of this segment is that something isn't right. The hero isn't living the life he wants to live, even if he can't quite put his finger on why.

Then, something happens to shake the hero out of their stupor: an unexpected event that pushes them out of their comfort zone and kicks off a metamorphosis. They may be resistant to the changes in their life at first, and they may or may not come upon a mentor-like figure who will guide them through their transformation.

Now the stage is set, the ball sent rolling, and the journey begun.

Soon, the hero eases into their new circumstances and starts to make some small gains on their position in the world.

But almost equally as soon come's an event Campbell calls "crossing the threshold." Here the hero's commitment to the long journey before them is put to the test. Here they must conquer some "unknown" challenge that arises.

The successful "crossing of the threshold" concludes Act One. Now, the training wheels have been removed and there's no going back for our hero.

ACT TWO: In the next leg of the journey, our hero begins to see some real progress towards their goal. Now they start to become real "players" in the game of their endeavor, so to speak. New allies are met, and new challenges arise which the hero overcomes.

But just when things are starting to look like gravy, "the ordeal" rears its ugly head. The ordeal is an elephant-sized problem that makes Act One's threshold look like small potatoes. It shatters the hero and appears to undo everything they've gained so far.

Now, the audience spends some significant time with the hero at his or her worst. They feel the hero's pain.

Act Two concludes with the hero at his lowest point yet, questioning whether they would have been better off if they never embarked on the journey to begin with. If the hero had a mentor figure in the story, they've most likely lost access to his or her valuable guidance by this point.

ACT THREE: The final act revives the plot with a spark of inspiration that carries the hero out of their despair. Here something almost magical occurs that prompts our protagonist to resume their noble cause.

Back on the journey's path, the hero—having suffered great injury from Act Two's ordeal—finds progress more difficult than ever. Every inch forward is a battle, but their strength of spirit has returned, and the audience is rooting for them every step of the way.

At this point, the hero might need to attain some form of hidden knowledge or power that will allow them to triumph over the ordeal. Here, a second transformation occurs: a re-forging and redoubling of the first great change that set them on their path to begin with.

This prepares the hero for their final confrontation with the ordeal.

But what sort of dramatic confrontation would it be if the hero's victory was assured? As the final conflict begins, the audience is made to realize that the ordeal, too, has grown even more problematic since the hero's initial defeat, downfall, and hard-earned rebirth.

The hero now squares off against the "supreme ordeal" here at the ultimate climax of the story, and the stakes have never been higher.

The hero, of course, comes out of the finale triumphant. But their triumph is probably bitter-sweet, as they've most likely lost something very dear to them in the process of overcoming their ordeal. Overall, however, their end goal has been achieved, and their long and difficult transformation a success.

Finally, the hero returns to their place of origin—a changed and better person—and share the spoils of their victory with the less fortunate. And so, the hero's journey ends—in a sense—exactly where it began, and the cycle is complete.

A Very Simple Example of the Monomyth in Action

See now, how the monomyth can be harnessed to deliver a seemingly mundane happening as though it were a life-changing sequence of events—all leading up to a profound and memorable conclusion...

ACT ONE: I'd been working 50 hour weeks at the office for five years straight. My eyes felt like they were about to fall out of their sockets for lack of natural sunlight.

Driving home one day, those tired eyes of mine saw the cutest baby squirrel on the side of the road...flattened like a pancake. I saw that, and that's when it hit me. Our time on this earth is just too short. I decided that I needed to get out of the office and clear my head. Center myself. Figure out what I'm doing with my life.

I booked a spot on a nearby campground for the weekend. Just me and the great outdoors for 48 hours straight.

But naturally, my boss paid a visit to my cubicle on the Friday before my trip.

"We need you here for the Peterman account this weekend," he said. "I hate to ask again, but I know we can always count on you for— "

"—NO." I cut him off, eyes bulging. Beneath my desk, I could feel my hands balling up into fists.

My boss looked absolutely thunderstruck.

"NO." I told him again. He looked at me. I looked at him. I must have looked like a crazy person, because he didn't say another word. He just backed on out of the cubicle and went his way.

ACT TWO: The first couple hours of roughing it were great. I hit the trails right away—went for a nice, long walk. I breathed in clean, fresh air; stretched out all my aching muscles. Already, I was starting to feel like a whole new person.

But then night fell, and disaster struck.

Turns out I'd locked my keys in the car. Not just my keys, mind you, everything. My cell phone. My tent. All my food and other essentials. Just a

Just then, I heard a *crack* in the distance. Thunder. Clouds had rolled in out of nowhere. In the next second, it was pouring down rain.

And what do you know what else? It just so happened this one of the last weekends that the campground was open for the season, and the whole place was practically abandoned.

I hiked a good two miles from where I was parked to the front help station, only to find that this post was just as empty as everywhere else. Great customer service, right?

All I could think to do was take shelter in the woods, and even that hardly helped, it was raining so hard. Freezing, soaked, huddled up in a ball against a big rotting stump, all I could think about was what a dummy I had been.

 Right now, I could have been heading home from the office for an evening of nice, dry, temperature-controlled modern shelter.

Instead I was crouched here like an animal at the world's worst campground. I thought, *how did I get this stupid camping idea into my head?*

ACT THREE: At some point I must have fallen asleep there in the woods. When I woke up, it was still dark, but at least the rain had stopped. The moon must have been about full that night because I could still make out the trail just fine.

I knew I needed to get moving or I'd probably catch pneumonia from sitting their soaked clothing. Should I go back to my car and try to bust the window open? I decided that I would go further along the trail, keeping an eye out for a suitable rock to do the job.

I kept up along the trial for some time, toes growing numb in my shoes, until I came unto to a big muddy pond. It was the campground's fishing hole I guess. I plopped down on a log to rest for a while before I headed back. And just when I did, that's when it happened. A moment in time that would change my life forever.

The sun rose.

All at once those golden, pink and orange hues started dancing on the dirty, mucky pond. Lit it up like a canvas of neon. And while this pond is transforming into something wonderful—

while I'm sitting here on a log, haven't eaten in a day, covered in mud, eyes dried up like some raisins because I slept in my contacts...all I'm thinking is: this is so...beautiful.

And then I realize, I've never done this. I've never watched a sunrise. Not once. Not even when I was kid. My dad wasn't the type to take us on early morning fishing trips, he was too busy...working...

...but hell, who am I to hold that against him? When he was my age he already had a wife and kids. Me? I've been too busy working to even get that much out of life...

So there I am, looking out at the most beautiful sunset I've ever seen (the only one I've seen, to be fair), filthy and tired here at the world's worst campground, thinking all these things…and I start to tear up. But you know what? They're tears of joy.

Because now I feel like some curse has been lifted. Now I feel awake. And as I head back to my campground, I'm not worried about my situation with my car, because all I can think is "What else have I missed?

What other beautiful things have been under my nose this whole time, things that I've been too busy working to appreciate?"

So I get back to my car and you know what's the first thing I see? Something shiny embedded in the dirt by my tire. I didn't lock my keys in my car, I missed dropping them in my pocket.

Why had I not noticed? Because I was too busy with the task of *unbusying* myself when I got out of the car for the weekend.

I called in sick that Monday. Took the next Friday off, then following week entirely. I read some books I had been meaning to read for years. I went out. Made new friends.

Then I came back to work more refreshed than any weekend in the woods by itself could have done for me.

And the first thing I told my boss when I got back? I told him how we ought to have a company camping trip.

Making the Monomyth Work for You

You've just read but one, very quick, very loose example of the monomyth in action.

I'm sure you noticed that the story hardly followed the monomyth to a T. There was no mentor involved, nor did the plot's ordeal up the ante toward the end of our hero's journey.

Still, the broad brush strokes of the journey were there, and the made what could have been an entirely uninteresting story into something impactful.

Once you've memorized the beats of the monomythic hero's journey, you start to see it everywhere. In modern fiction. In TV and movies. Even on a micro scale in commercials, print ads, and product branding.

Once you've absorbed the monomyth completely, you'll start to wonder how it's possible to tell a good story *without it*. It works so well, perhaps, because it's the most obvious way of structuring a meaningful plot.

As I said before, there are no rules when it comes to speech writing, only guidelines. So, too, is the structure of the monomyth nothing more than an effective set of guidelines for telling stories to your audience. Feel free to add your own flair to the formula, but there's also no need to reinvent the wheel.

Chapter 3 – The Power of the Senses: Using Words To Paint Pictures in Your Audience's Heads

There's a saying when it comes to story writing: show, don't tell. That means, instead of telling your reader outright that so-and-so is a *bad guy*, write a scene in which his actions reveal his lack of moral fiber instead.

When your story *telling*, the principle remains the same.

In last chapter's example monomyth, the speaker does more than just *telling* his audience that the sunrise was something beautiful. Instead, he first lets them reach that conclusion on their own.

He describes the lovely colors that he saw that morning, painting a picture of a lovely sunrise for his audience to enjoy in their own mind's eye.

Likewise, in the midst of his "ordeal," he never outright tells the audience that he's miserable. Instead, he tells them certain details that add up to form the picture of a miserable person.

If you want to really connect with your audience, this is how it's done. The less selfless you are in your manner of storytelling, the better. Literally share *your experience* **with the audience.**

Research shows that after just a few minutes of passive observation, a person's brain switches over into the "alpha" state of mind. In this state, a listener's subconscious is "exposed" and they are much more vulnerable to suggestion.

Their higher functions or reasoning and critical thinking are diminished, their guard is let down, and—at least, initially—they're along for the ride whether they like it or not. It's your job to keep them in that state with plenty of passive brain stimulation.

How to do that? With good storytelling, of course. More specifically, with *vivid* storytelling that stimulates your audience's imaginations. When their imaginations are engaged, they'll be less critical of your message, and they'll also be more open to new ideas.

While relaying your story, give each audience member's senses something to chew on. Again, share *your experience*. Tell them how you broke out into goosebumps. How your stomach dropped. How a chill ran up your spine.

Pepper your narrative with sensory-rich statements such as these, and you're guaranteed to captivate your audience on a whole new level.

Some Simple but Effective Sensory-Rich Angles to Consider:

- Describe physical reactions that you had to the event. "I just blinked." "My stomach dropped." "My throat closed up." This is a powerful tactic for putting the listener in your shoes.

Everybody's experienced these involuntary physical reactions at some point in their lives. Your audience's mind, therefore, is already wired to associate these things with certain stimuli.

- Talk about what your hands or other parts of your body were doing while the event was taking place. Don't tell them you were mad, tell them how your hands balled up into fists.

  Don't say you were afraid, talk about how you could feel your fingers trembling. Don't say that a person in the story looked impatient, describe how they were tapping their foot on the ground at sixty miles per hour.

- Experiment with the present tense as you tell your story. You may have noticed that the example monomyth shifted tense like this towards the peak of the message. Such a change is much less obvious in a verbal presentation.

  Don't say "and then our boat went under," describe the process of your shipwreck as if it were unfolding before your eyes right now.

  Talk about how you "look down and there's water up to your ankles out of nowhere." Act as if whatever you're talking about was going on in the present.

  This is another useful technique for inserting your audience into the cockpit of your story.

Conclusion

You've just learned about the monomyth—the ancestral root of virtually all modern storytelling—and how to use it to go about telling your tales in a more impactful fashion.

You've also learned about using sensory-rich language to make your tales more "vivid." You've also received a quick crash course on how to conduct your public speaking performance like an old pro.

In short, you've been handed all the tools you need for high-level oral storytelling. Now it's up to you to put those tools to work.

Put the monomyth into action, use sensory-rich angles to unravel your plot, and get your message out there on an emotional level via the power of symbolic representation.

Never forget, nobody can offer an audience what you have to offer them. Your message, your story, your perspective—these are all things unique to you as an individual. Trust in yourself, and the process will be as impactful and life-changing to you as your final product will be to the audience.

www.ingramcontent.com/pod-product-compliance
Lightning Source LLC
Chambersburg PA
CBHW070422190526
45169CB00003B/1372